ETERNAL LIFE

With an Essay on
Eternity
By John Charles Ryle

By

HENRY DRUMMOND

First published in 1896

This edition published by Read Books Ltd.
Copyright © 2019 Read Books Ltd.
This book is copyright and may not be
reproduced or copied in any way without
the express permission of the publisher in writing

British Library Cataloguing-in-Publication Data
A catalogue record for this book is available
from the British Library

CONTENTS

ETERNITY..5

ETERNAL LIFE....................................21

ETERNITY

An Extract from *Practical Religion* By John Charles Ryle

"*The things which are seen are temporal; but the things which are not seen are eternal.*"

—2 Cor. iv. 18.

A subject stands out on the face of this text which is one of the most solemn and heart-searching in the Bible. That subject is *eternity*.

The subject is one of which the wisest man can only take in a little. We have no eyes to see it fully, no line to fathom it, no mind to grasp it; and yet we must not refuse to consider it. There are star-depths in the heavens above us, which the most powerful telescope cannot pierce; yet it is well to look into them and learn something, if we cannot learn everything. There are heights and depths about the subject of eternity which mortal man can never comprehend; but God has spoken of it, and we have no right to turn away from it altogether.

The subject is one which we must never approach without the Bible in our hands. The moment we depart from "God's Word written," in considering eternity and the future state of man, we are likely to fall into error. In examining points like these we have nothing to do with preconceived notions as to what is God's character, and what *we think* God ought to be, or ought to do with man after death. We have only to find out what is written. What saith the Scripture? What saith the Lord? It is wild work to tell us that we ought to have "noble thoughts about God," independent of, and over and above, Scripture. Natural religion soon comes to a standstill here. The noblest thoughts about God which we have a right to hold are the thoughts which He has been pleased to reveal to us in His "written Word."

I ask the attention of all into whose hands this paper may fall, while I offer a few suggestive thoughts about eternity. As a mortal man I feel deeply my own insufficiency to handle this subject. But I pray that God the Holy Ghost, whose strength is made perfect in weakness, may bless the words I speak, and make them seeds of eternal life in many minds.

I.

The first thought which I commend to the attention of my readers is this:—*We live in a world where all things are temporal and passing away.*

That man must be blind indeed who cannot realize this. Everything around us is decaying, dying, and coming to an end. There is a sense no doubt in which "matter" is eternal. Once created, it will never entirely perish. But in a popular practical sense, there is nothing undying about us except our souls. No wonder the poet says:—

"Change and decay in all around I see:
O Thou that changest not, abide with me!"

We are all going, going, going, whether high or low, gentle or simple, rich or poor, old or young. We are all going, and shall soon be gone.

Beauty is only temporal. Sarah was once the fairest of women, and the admiration of the Court of Egypt; yet a day came when even Abraham, her husband, said, "Let me bury my dead out of my sight." (Gen. xxiii. 4.)—Strength of body is only temporal.

David was once a mighty man of valour, the slayer of the lion and the bear, and the champion of Israel against Goliath; yet a day came when even David had to be nursed and ministered to in his old age like a child.—Wisdom and power of brain are only temporal. Solomon was once a prodigy of knowledge, and all the kings of the earth came to hear his wisdom; yet even Solomon in his latter days played the fool exceedingly, and allowed his wives to "turn away his heart." (1 Kings xi. 2.)

Humbling and painful as these truths may sound, it is good for us all to realize them and lay them to heart. The houses we live in, the homes we love, the riches we accumulate, the professions we follow, the plans we form, the relations we enter into,—they are only for a time. "The things seen are temporal." "The fashion of this world passeth away." (1 Cor. vii. 31.)

The thought is one which ought to rouse every one who is living only for this world. If his conscience is not utterly seared, it should stir in him great searchings of heart. Oh, take care what you are doing! Awake to see things in their true light before it be too late. The things you live for now are all temporal and passing away. The pleasures, the amusements, the recreations, merrymakings, the profits, the earthly callings, which now absorb all your heart and drink up all your mind, will soon be over. They are poor ephemeral things which cannot last. Oh, love them not too well; grasp them not too tightly; make them not your idols! You cannot keep them, and you must leave them. Seek first the kingdom of God, and then everything else shall be added to you. "Set your affections on things above, not on things on the earth." Oh, you that love the world, be wise in time! Never, never forget that it is written, "The world passeth away, and the lust thereof; but he that doeth the will of God abideth for ever." (Col. iii. 2; 1 John ii. 17.)

The same thought ought to cheer and comfort every true Christian. Your trials, crosses, and conflicts, are all temporal. They will soon have an end; and even now they are working for you "a far more exceeding and eternal weight of glory." (2 Cor.

iv. 17.) Take them patiently: bear them quietly: look upward, forward, onward, and far beyond them. Fight your daily fight under an abiding conviction that it is only for a little time, and that rest is not far off. Carry your daily cross with an abiding recollection that it is one of the "things seen" which are temporal. The cross shall soon be exchanged for a crown, and you shall sit down with Abraham, Isaac, and Jacob in the kingdom of God.

II.

The second thought which I commend to the attention of my readers is this:—*We are all going towards a world where everything is eternal.*

That great unseen state of existence which lies behind the grave, is for ever. Whether it be happy or miserable, whether it be a condition of joy or sorrow, in one respect it is utterly unlike this world,—it is for ever. *There* at any rate will be no change and decay, no end, no good-bye, no mornings and evenings, no alteration, no annihilation. Whatever there is beyond the tomb, when the last trumpet has sounded, and the dead are raised, will be endless, everlasting, and eternal. "The things unseen are eternal."

We cannot fully realize this condition. The contrast between now and then, between this world and the next, is so enormously great that our feeble minds will not take it in. The consequences it entails are so tremendous, that they almost take away our breath, and we shrink from looking at them. But when the Bible speaks plainly we have no right to turn away from a subject, and with the Bible in our hands we shall do well to look at the "things which are eternal."

Let us settle it then in our minds, for one thing, that the *future happiness* of those who are saved is eternal. However little we may understand it, it is something which will have no end: it will never cease, never grow old, never decay, never die. At

God's "right hand are pleasures for evermore." (Ps. xvi. 11.) Once landed in paradise, the saints of God shall go out no more. The inheritance is "incorruptible, undefiled, and fadeth not away." They shall "receive a crown of glory that fadeth not away." (1 Pet. i. 4; v. 4.) Their warfare is accomplished; their fight is over; their work is done. They shall hunger no more, neither thirst any more. They are travelling on towards an "eternal weight of glory," towards a home which shall never be broken up, a meeting without a parting, a family gathering without a separation, a day without night. Faith shall be swallowed up in sight, and hope in certainty. They shall see as they have been seen, and know as they have been known, and "be for ever with the Lord." I do not wonder that the apostle Paul adds, "Comfort one another with these words." (1 Thess. iv. 17, 18.)

Let us settle it, for another thing, in our minds, that the *future misery* of those who are finally lost is eternal. This is an awful truth, I am aware, and flesh and blood naturally shrink from the contemplation of it. But I am one of those who believe it to be plainly revealed in Scripture, and I dare not keep it back in the pulpit. To my eyes eternal future happiness and eternal future misery appear to stand side by side. I fail to see how you can distinguish the duration of one from the duration of the other. If the joy of the believer is for ever, the sorrow of the unbeliever is also for ever. If heaven is eternal, so likewise is hell. It may be my ignorance, but I know not how the conclusion can be avoided.

I cannot reconcile the non-eternity of punishment with the *language of the Bible*. Its advocates talk loudly about love and charity, and say that it does not harmonize with the merciful and compassionate character of God. But what saith the Scripture? Who ever spoke such loving and merciful words as our Lord Jesus Christ? Yet His are the lips which three times over describe the consequence of impenitence and sin, as "the worm that never dies and the fire that is not quenched." He is the Person who speaks in one sentence of the wicked going away into "everlasting punishment" and the righteous into "life eternal." (Mark ix. 43—

48; Matt. xxv. 46.)—Who does not remember the Apostle Paul's words about charity? Yet he is the very Apostle who says, the wicked "shall be punished with everlasting destruction." (2 Thess. i. 9.)—Who does not know the spirit of love which runs through all St. John's Gospel and Epistles? Yet the beloved Apostle is the very writer in the New Testament who dwells most strongly, in the book of Revelation, on the reality and eternity of future woe. What shall we say to these things? Shall we be wise above that which is written? Shall we admit the dangerous principle that words in Scripture do not mean what they appear to mean? Is it not far better to lay our hands on our mouths and say, "Whatever God has written must be true." "Even so, Lord God Almighty, true and righteous are Thy judgments." (Rev. xvi. 7.)

I cannot reconcile the non-eternity of punishment with the *language of our Prayer-book*. The very first petition in our matchless Litany contains this sentence, "From everlasting damnation, good Lord, deliver us."—The Catechism teaches every child who learns it, that whenever we repeat the Lord's Prayer we desire our Heavenly Father to "keep us from our ghostly enemy and from everlasting death."—Even in our Burial Service we pray at the grave side, "Deliver us not into the bitter pains of eternal death."—Once more I ask, "What shall we say to these things?" Shall our congregations be taught that even when people live and die in sin we may hope for their happiness in a remote future? Surely the common sense of many of our worshippers would reply, that if this is the case Prayer-book words mean nothing at all.

I lay no claim to any peculiar knowledge of Scripture. I feel daily that I am no more infallible than the Bishop of Rome. But I must speak according to the light which God has given to me; and I do not think I should do my duty if I did not raise a warning voice on this subject, and try to put Christians on their guard. Six thousand years ago sin entered into the world by the devil's daring falsehood,—"Ye shall not surely die." (Gen. iii. 4.) At the end of six thousand years the great enemy of mankind is still using his old weapon, and trying to persuade men that they may live and die in sin, and yet at some distant period may be finally saved. Let us not be ignorant of his devices. Let us walk steadily in the old paths. Let us hold fast the old truth, and believe that as the happiness of the saved is eternal, so also is the misery of the lost.

> (a) Let us hold it fast *in the interest of the whole system of revealed religion.* What was the use of God's Son becoming incarnate, agonizing in Gethsemane, and dying on the cross to make atonement, if men can be finally saved without believing on Him? Where is the slightest proof that saving faith in Christ's blood can ever begin after death? Where is the need of the Holy Ghost, if sinners are at last to enter heaven without conversion and renewal of heart? Where can we find the smallest evidence that any one can be born again, and have a new heart, if he dies in an unregenerate state? If a man may escape eternal punishment at last, without faith in Christ or sanctification of the Spirit, sin is no longer an infinite evil, and there was no need for Christ making an atonement.

> (b) Let us hold it fast *for the sake of holiness and morality.* I can imagine nothing so pleasant to flesh and blood as the specious theory that we may live in sin, and yet escape eternal perdition; and that although we "serve divers lusts and pleasures" while we are here, we shall somehow or other all get to heaven hereafter! Only tell the young man who is "wasting his substance in riotous living" that there is heaven at last even for those who live and die in sin, and he is never likely to turn from evil. Why should he repent and take up the cross, if he can get to heaven at last without trouble?

(c) Finally, let us hold it fast, *for the sake of the common hopes of all God's saints.* Let us distinctly understand that every blow struck at the eternity of punishment is an equally heavy blow at the eternity of reward. It is impossible to separate the two things. No ingenious theological definition can divide them. They stand or fall together. The same language is used, the same figures of speech are employed, when the Bible speaks about either condition. Every attack on the duration of hell is also an attack on the duration of heaven. It is a deep and true saying, "With the sinner's fear our hope departs."

I turn from this part of my subject with a deep sense of its painfulness. I feel strongly with Robert M'Cheyne, that "it is a hard subject to handle lovingly." But I turn from it with an equally deep conviction that if we believe the Bible we must never give up anything which it contains. From hard, austere, and unmerciful theology, good Lord, deliver us! If men are not saved it is because they "will not come to Christ." (John v. 40.) But we must not be wise above that which is written. No morbid love of liberality, so called, must induce us to reject anything which God has revealed about eternity. Men sometimes talk exclusively about God's mercy and love and compassion, as if He had no other attributes, and leave out of sight entirely His holiness and His purity, His justice and His unchangeableness, and His hatred of sin. Let us beware of falling into this delusion. It is a growing evil in these latter days. Low and inadequate views of the unutterable vileness and filthiness of sin, and of the unutterable purity of the eternal God, are fertile sources of error about man's future state. Let us think of the mighty Being with whom we have to do, as he Himself declared His character to Moses, saying, "The Lord, the Lord God, merciful and gracious, long-suffering and abundant in goodness and truth, keeping mercy for thousands, forgiving iniquity, and transgression and sin." But let us not forget the solemn clause which concludes the sentence: "And *that will by no means clear the guilty.*" (Exod. xxxiv. 6, 7.) Unrepented sin is an eternal evil, and can never cease to be sin; and He with whom we have to do is an eternal God.

The words of Psalm cxlv. are strikingly beautiful: "The Lord is gracious, and full of compassion; slow to anger, and of great mercy. The Lord is good to all: and His tender mercies are over all His works.—The Lord upholdeth all that fall, and raiseth up all those that be bowed down.—The Lord is righteous in all His ways, and holy in all His works. The Lord is nigh unto all them that call upon Him, to all that call upon Him in truth.—The Lord preserveth all them that love Him." Nothing can exceed the mercifulness of this language! But what a striking fact it is that the passage goes on to add the following solemn conclusion, "*All the wicked will He destroy.*" (Psalm cxlv. 8-20.)

III.

The third thought which I commend to the attention of my readers is this:—*Our state in the unseen world of eternity depends entirely on what we are in time.*

The life that we live upon earth is short at the very best, and soon gone. "We spend our days as a tale that is told."—"What is our life? It is a vapour: so soon passeth it away, and we are gone." (Psalm xc. 9; James iv. 14.) The life that is before us when we leave this world is an endless eternity, a sea without a bottom, and an ocean without a shore. "One day in Thy sight," eternal God, "is as a thousand years, and a thousand years as one day." (2 Pet. iii. 8.) In that world time shall be no more.—But short as our life is here, and endless as it will be hereafter, it is a tremendous thought that eternity hinges upon time. Our lot after death depends, humanly speaking, on what we are while we are alive. It is written, God "will render to every man according to his deeds: to them who by patient continuance in well-doing seek for glory and honour and immortality, eternal life: but to them that are contentious, and do not obey the truth, but obey unrighteousness, indignation and wrath." (Rom. ii. 6, 7.)

We ought never to forget, that we are all, while we live, in a state of probation. We are constantly sowing seeds which will spring up and bear fruit, every day and hour in our lives. There are eternal consequences resulting from all our thoughts and words and actions, of which we take far too little account. "For every idle word that men speak they shall give account in the day of judgment." (Matt. xii. 36.) Our thoughts are all numbered, our actions are weighed. No wonder that St. Paul says, "He that soweth to the flesh shall of the flesh reap corruption; but he that soweth to the Spirit shall of the Spirit reap life everlasting." (Gal. vi. 8.) In a word, what we sow in life we shall reap after death, and reap to all eternity.

There is no greater delusion than the common idea that it is possible to live wickedly, and yet rise again gloriously; to be without religion in this world, and yet to be a saint in the next. When the famous Whitefield revived the doctrine of conversion last century, it is reported that one of his hearers came to him after a sermon and said,—"It is all quite true, sir. I hope I shall be converted and born again one day, but not till after I am dead." I fear there are many like him. I fear the false doctrine of the Romish *purgatory* has many secret friends even within the pale of the Church of England! However carelessly men may go on while they live, they secretly cling to the hope that they shall be found among the saints when they die. They seem to hug the idea that there is some cleansing, purifying effect produced by death, and that, whatever they may be in this life, they shall be found "meet for the inheritance of the saints" in the life to come. But it is all a delusion.

"Life is the time to serve the Lord,
The time to insure the great reward."

 The Bible teaches plainly, that as we die, whether converted or unconverted, whether believers or unbelievers, whether godly or ungodly, so shall we rise again when the last trumpet sounds. There is no repentance in the grave: there is no conversion after the last breath is drawn. Now is the time to believe in Christ, and to lay hold on eternal life. Now is the time to turn from darkness unto light, and to make our calling and election sure. The night cometh when no man can work. As the tree falls, there it will lie. If we leave this world impenitent and unbelieving, we shall rise the same in the resurrection morning, and find it had been "good for us if we had never been born."
 I charge every reader of this paper to remember this, and to make a good use of time. Regard it as the stuff of which life is made, and never waste it or throw it away. Your hours and days and weeks and months and years have all something to say to an eternal condition beyond the grave. What you sow in life you are sure to reap in a life to come. As holy Baxter says, it is "now or never." Whatever we do in religion must be done now.
 Remember this in your use of all the means of grace, from the least to the greatest. Never be careless about them. They are given to be your helps toward an eternal world, and not one of them ought to be thoughtlessly treated or lightly and irreverently handled. Your daily prayers and Bible-reading, your weekly behaviour on the Lord's day, your manner of going through public worship,—all, all these things are important. Use them all as one who remembers eternity.
 Remember it, not least, whenever you are tempted to do evil. When sinners entice you, and say, "It is only a little one,"—when Satan whispers in your heart, "Never mind: where is the mighty harm? Everybody does so,"—then look beyond time to a world unseen, and place in the face of the temptation the thought of eternity. There is a grand saying recorded of the martyred

Reformer, Bishop Hooper, when one urged him to recant before he was burned, saying, "Life is sweet and death is bitter." "True," said the good Bishop, "quite true! But eternal life is more sweet, and eternal death is more bitter."

IV.

The last thought which I commend to the attention of my readers is this:—*The Lord Jesus Christ is the great Friend to whom we must all look for help, both for time and eternity.*

The purpose for which the eternal Son of God came into the world can never be declared too fully, or proclaimed too loudly. He came to give us hope and peace while we live among the "things seen, which are temporal," and glory and blessedness when we go into the "things unseen, which are eternal." He came to "bring life and immortality to light," and to "deliver those who, through fear of death, were all their life-time subject to bondage." (2 Tim. i. 10; Heb. ii. 15.) He saw our lost and bankrupt condition, and had compassion on us. And now, blessed be His name, a mortal man may pass through "things temporal" with comfort, and look forward to "things eternal" without fear.

These mighty privileges our Lord Jesus Christ has purchased for us at the cost of His own precious blood. He became our Substitute, and bore our sins in His own body on the cross, and then rose again for our justification. "He suffered for sins, the just for the unjust, that He might bring us unto God." He was made sin for us who knew no sin, that we poor sinful creatures might have pardon and justification while we live, and glory and blessedness when we die. (1 Peter ii. 24; iii. 18; 2 Cor. v. 21.)

And all that our Lord Jesus Christ has purchased for us He offers freely to every one who will turn from his sins, come to Him, and believe. "I am the light of the world," He says: "he that followeth Me shall not walk in darkness, but shall have the light of life."—"Come unto Me, all ye that labour and are heavy laden, and I will give you rest."—"If any man thirst, let him come unto Me and drink."—"Him that cometh unto Me I will in no wise cast out."—And the terms are as simple as the offer is free: "Believe on the Lord Jesus Christ and thou shalt be saved."—"Whosoever believeth on Him shall not perish but have eternal life." (John viii. 12; Matt. xi. 28; John vii. 37; vi. 37; Acts xvi. 31; John iii. 16.)

He that has Christ, has life. He can look round him on the "things temporal," and see change and decay on every side without dismay. He has got treasure in heaven, which neither rust nor moth can corrupt, nor thieves break through and steal. He can look forward to the "things eternal," and feel calm and composed. His Saviour has risen, and gone to prepare a place for him. When he leaves this world he shall have a crown of glory, and be for ever with his Lord. He can look down even into the grave, as the wisest Greeks and Romans could never do, and say, "Oh, death, where is thy sting? oh, grave, where is thy victory? oh, eternity, where are thy terrors?" (1 Cor. xv. 55.)

Let us all settle it firmly in our minds that the only way to pass through "things seen" with comfort, and look forward to "things unseen" without fear, is to have Christ for our Saviour and Friend, to lay hold on Christ by faith, to become one with Christ and Christ in us, and while we live in the flesh to live the life of faith in the Son of God. (Gal. ii. 20.) How vast is the difference between the state of him who has faith in Christ, and the state of him who has none! Blessed indeed is that man or woman who can say, with truth, "I trust in Jesus: I believe." When Cardinal Beaufort lay upon his death-bed, our mighty poet describes King Henry as saying, "He dies, but gives no sign." When John Knox, the Scotch Reformer, was drawing to his end, and unable to speak, a faithful servant asked him to give some proof that the Gospel he had preached in life gave him comfort in death, by raising his hand. He heard; and raised his hand toward heaven three times, and then departed. Blessed, I say again, is he that believes! He alone is rich, independent, and beyond the reach of harm. If you and I have no comfort amidst things temporal, and no hope for the things eternal, the fault is all our own. It is because we "will not come to Christ, that we may have life." (John v. 40.)

I leave the subject of eternity here, and pray that God may bless it to many souls. In conclusion, I offer to every one who reads this volume some food for thought, and matter for self-examination.

(1) First of all, how are you *using your time*? Life is short and very uncertain. You never know what a day may bring forth. Business and pleasure, money-getting and money-spending, eating and drinking, marrying and giving in marriage,—all, all will soon be over and done with for ever. And you, what are you doing for your immortal soul? Are you wasting time, or turning it to good account? Are you preparing to meet God?

(2) Secondly, where *shall you be in eternity*? It is coming, coming, coming very fast upon us. You are going, going, going very fast into it. But where will you be? On the right hand or on the left, in the day of judgment? Among the lost or among the saved? Oh, rest not, rest not till your soul is insured! Make sure work: leave nothing uncertain. It is a fearful thing to die unprepared, and fall into the hands of the living God.

(3) Thirdly, would you be *safe for time and eternity*? Then seek Christ, and believe in Him. Come to Him just as you are. Seek Him while He may be found, call upon Him while He is near. There is still a throne of grace. It is not too late. Christ waits to be gracious: He invites you to come to Him. Before the door is shut and the judgment begins, repent, believe, and be saved.

(4) Lastly, *would you be happy*? Cling to Christ, and live the life of faith in Him. Abide in Him, and live near to Him.

Follow Him with heart and soul and mind and strength, and seek to know Him better every day. So doing you shall have great peace while you pass through "things temporal," and in the midst of a dying world shall "never die." (John xi. 26.) So doing, you shall be able to look forward to "things eternal" with unfailing confidence, and to feel and "know that if our earthly house of this tabernacle be dissolved we have a building of God, a house not made with hands, eternal in the heavens." (2 Cor. v. 1.)

ETERNAL LIFE.

"This is Life Eternal—that they might know Thee, the True God, and Jesus Christ whom Thou has sent."

—*Jesus Christ.*

"Perfect correspondence would be perfect life. Were there no changes in the environment but such as the organism had adapted changes to meet, and were it never to fail in the efficiency with which it met them, there would be eternal existence and eternal knowledge."

—*Herbert Spencer.*

ONE of the most startling achievements of recent science is a definition of Eternal Life. To the religious mind this is a contribution of immense moment. For eighteen hundred years only one definition of Life Eternal was before the world. Now there are two.

Through all these centuries revealed religion had this doctrine to itself. Ethics had a voice, as well as Christianity, on the question of the *summum bonum*; Philosophy ventured to speculate on the Being of a God. But no source outside Christianity contributed anything to the doctrine of Eternal Life. Apart from Revelation, this great truth was unguaranteed. It was the one thing in the Christian system that most needed verification from without, yet none was forthcoming. And never has any further light been thrown upon the question why in its very nature the Christian Life should be Eternal. Christianity itself even upon this point has been obscure. Its decision upon the bare fact is authoritative and specific. But as to what there is in the Spiritual Life necessarily endowing it with the element of Eternity, the maturest theology is all but silent.

It has been reserved for modern biology at once to defend and illuminate this central truth of the Christian faith. And hence in the interests of religion, practical and evidential, this second and scientific definition of Eternal Life is to be hailed as an announcement of commanding interest. Why it should not yet have received the recognition of religious thinkers—for already it has lain some years unnoticed—is not difficult to understand. The belief in Science as an aid to faith is not yet ripe enough to warrant men in searching there for witnesses to the highest Christian truths. The inspiration of Nature, it is thought, extends to the humbler doctrines alone. And yet the reverent inquirer who guides his steps in the right direction may find even now in the still dim twilight of the scientific world much that will illuminate and intensify his sublimest faith. Here, at least, comes, and comes unbidden, the opportunity of testing the most vital point of the Christian system. Hitherto the Christian philosopher has remained content with the scientific evidence against Annihilation. Or, with Butler, he has reasoned from the Metamorphoses of Insects to a future life. Or again, with the authors of "The Unseen Universe," the apologist has constructed elaborate, and certainly impressive, arguments upon the Law of Continuity. But now we may draw nearer. For the first time Science touches Christianity *positively* on the doctrine of Immortality. It confronts us with an actual definition of an Eternal Life, based on a full and rigidly accurate examination of the necessary conditions. Science does not pretend that it can fulfil these conditions. Its votaries make no claim to possess the Eternal Life. It simply postulates the requisite conditions without concerning itself whether any organism should ever appear, or does now exist, which might fulfil them. The claim of religion, on the other hand, is that there are organisms which possess Eternal Life. And the problem for us to solve is this: Do those who profess to possess Eternal Life fulfil the conditions required by Science, or are they different conditions? In a word, Is the Christian conception of Eternal Life scientific?

It may be unnecessary to notice at the outset that the definition of Eternal Life drawn up by Science was framed without reference to religion. It must indeed have been the last thought with the thinker to whom we chiefly owe it, that in unfolding the conception of a Life in its very nature necessarily eternal, he was contributing to Theology.

Mr. Herbert Spencer—for it is to him we owe it—would be the first to admit the impartiality of his definition; and from the connection in which it occurs in his writings, it is obvious that religion was not even present to his mind. He is analyzing with minute care the relations between Environment and Life. He unfolds the principle according to which Life is high or low, long or short. He shows why organisms live and why they die. And finally he defines a condition of things in which an organism would never die—in which it would enjoy a perpetual and perfect Life. This to him is, of course, but a speculation. Life Eternal is a biological conceit. The conditions necessary to an Eternal Life do not exist in the natural world. So that the definition is altogether impartial and independent. A Perfect Life, to Science, is simply a thing which is theoretically possible—like a Perfect Vacuum.

Before giving, in so many words, the definition of Mr. Herbert Spencer, it will render it fully intelligible if we gradually lead up to it by a brief rehearsal of the few and simple biological facts on which it is based. In considering the subject of Death, we have formerly seen that there are degrees of Life. By this is meant that some lives have more and fuller correspondence with Environment than others. The amount of correspondence, again, is determined by the greater or less complexity of the organism. Thus a simple organism like the Amoeba is possessed of very few correspondences. It is a mere sac of transparent structureless jelly for which organization has done almost nothing, and hence it can only communicate with the smallest possible area of

Environment. An insect, in virtue of its more complex structure, corresponds with a wider area. Nature has endowed it with special faculties for reaching out to the Environment on many sides; it has more life than the Amoeba. In other words, it is a higher animal. Man again, whose body is still further differentiated, or broken up into different correspondences, finds himself *en rapport* with his surroundings to a further extent. And therefore he is higher still, more living still. And this law, that the degree of Life varies with the degree of correspondence, holds to the minutest detail throughout the entire range of living things. Life becomes fuller and fuller, richer and richer, more and more sensitive and responsive to an ever-widening Environment as we rise in the chain of being.

Now it will speedily appear that a distinct relation exists, and must exist, between complexity and longevity. Death being brought about by the failure of an organism to adjust itself to some change in the Environment, it follows that those organisms which are able to adjust themselves most readily and successfully will live the longest. They will continue time after time to effect the appropriate adjustment, and their power of doing so will be exactly proportionate to their complexity—that is, to the amount of Environment they can control with their correspondences. There are, for example, in the Environment of every animal certain things which are directly or indirectly dangerous to Life. If its equipment of correspondences is not complete enough to enable it to avoid these dangers in all possible circumstances, it must sooner or later succumb. The organism then with the most perfect set of correspondences, that is, the highest and most complex organism, has an obvious advantage over less complex forms. It can adjust itself more perfectly and frequently. But this is just the biological way of saying that it can live the longest. And hence the relation between complexity and longevity may be expressed thus—the most complex organisms are the longest lived.

To state and illustrate the proposition conversely may make

the point still further clear. The less highly organized an animal is, the less will be its chance of remaining in lengthened correspondence with its Environment. At some time or other in its career circumstances are sure to occur to which the comparatively immobile organism finds itself structurally unable to respond. Thus a *Medusa* tossed ashore by a wave, finds itself so out of correspondence with its new surroundings that its life must pay the forfeit. Had it been able by internal change to adapt itself to external change—to correspond sufficiently with the new environment, as for example to crawl, as an eel would have done, back into that environment with which it had completer correspondence—its life might have been spared. But had this happened it would continue to live henceforth only so long as it could continue in correspondence with all the circumstances in which it might find itself. Even if, however, it became complex enough to resist the ordinary and direct dangers of its environment, it might still be out of correspondence with others. A naturalist for instance, might take advantage of its want of correspondence with particular sights and sounds to capture it for his cabinet, or the sudden dropping of a yacht's anchor or the turn of a screw might cause its untimely death.

Again, in the case of a bird in virtue of its more complex organization, there is command over a much larger area of environment. It can take precautions such as the *Medusa* could not; it has increased facilities for securing food; its adjustments all round are more complex; and therefore it ought to be able to maintain its Life for a longer period. There is still a large area, however, over which it has no control. Its power of internal change is not complete enough to afford it perfect correspondence with all external changes, and its tenure of Life is to that extent insecure. Its correspondence, moreover, is limited even with regard to those external conditions with which it has been partially established. Thus a bird in ordinary circumstances has no difficulty in adapting itself to changes of temperature, but if these are varied beyond the point at which its capacity of adjustment begins to fail—for example, during an extreme winter—the organism being unable to meet the condition must perish. The human organism, on the other hand, can respond to this external condition, as well as to countless other vicissitudes under which lower forms would inevitably succumb. Man's adjustments are to the largest known area of Environment, and hence he ought to be able furthest to prolong his Life.

It becomes evident, then, that as we ascend in the scale of Life we rise also in the scale of longevity. The lowest organisms are, as a rule, shortlived, and the rate of mortality diminishes more or less regularly as we ascend in the animal scale. So extraordinary indeed is the mortality among lowly-organized forms that in most cases a compensation is actually provided, nature endowing them with a marvellously increased fertility in order to guard against absolute extinction. Almost all lower forms are furnished not only with great reproductive powers, but with different methods of propagation, by which, in various circumstances, and in an incredibly short time, the species can be indefinitely multiplied. Ehrenberg found that by the repeated subdivisions of a single *Paramecium*, no fewer than 268,000,000 similar organisms might be produced in one month. This power steadily decreases as we rise higher in the scale, until forms are reached in which one, two, or at most three, come into being at a birth. It decreases, however because it is no longer needed. These forms have a much longer lease of Life. And it may be taken as a rule, although it has exceptions, that complexity in animal organisms is always associated with longevity.

It may be objected that these illustrations are taken merely from morbid conditions. But whether the Life be cut short by accident or by disease the principle is the same. All dissolution is brought about practically in the same way. A certain condition in the Environment fails to be met by a corresponding condition in the organism, and this is death. And conversely the more an organism in virtue of its complexity can adapt itself to all the parts of its Environment, the longer it will live. "It is manifest *a priori*," says Mr. Herbert Spencer, "that since changes in the physical state of the environment, as also those mechanical actions and those variations of available food which occur in it, are liable to stop the processes going on in the organism; and since the adaptive changes in the organism have the effects of directly or indirectly counterbalancing these changes in the environment, it follows that the life of the organism will be short or long, low or high, according to the extent to which changes in the environment are met by corresponding changes in the organism. Allowing a margin for perturbations, the life will continue only while the correspondence continues; the completeness of the life will be proportionate to the completeness of the correspondence; and the life will be perfect only when the correspondence is perfect."[1]

We are now all but in sight of our scientific definition of Eternal Life. The desideratum is an organism with a correspondence of a very exceptional kind. It must lie beyond the reach of those "mechanical actions" and those "variations of available food," which are "liable to stop the processes going on in the organism." Before we reach an Eternal Life we must pass beyond that point at which all ordinary correspondences inevitably cease. We must find an organism so high and complex, that at some point in its development it shall have added a correspondence which organic death is powerless to arrest. We must, in short, pass beyond that finite region where the correspondences depend on evanescent and material media, and enter a further region where the Environment corresponded with is itself Eternal. Such an Environment exists. The Environment of the Spiritual world is outside the influence of these "mechanical actions," which sooner or later interrupt the processes going on in all finite organisms. If then we can find an organism which has established a correspondence with the spiritual world, that correspondence will possess the elements of eternity—provided only one other condition be fulfilled.

---

1 "Principles of Biology," p. 82.

That condition is that the Environment be perfect. If it is not perfect, if it is not the highest, if it is endowed with the finite quality of change, there can be no guarantee that the Life of its correspondents will be eternal. Some change might occur in it which the correspondents had no adaptive changes to meet, and Life would cease. But grant a spiritual organism in perfect correspondence with a perfect spiritual Environment, and the conditions necessary to Eternal Life are satisfied.

The exact terms of Mr. Herbert Spencer's definition of Eternal Life may now be given. And it will be seen that they include essentially the conditions here laid down. "Perfect correspondence would be perfect life. Were there no changes in the environment but such as the organism had adapted changes to meet, and were it never to fail in the efficiency with which it met them, there would be eternal existence and eternal knowledge."[2] Reserving the question as to the possible fulfilment of these conditions, let us turn for a moment to the definition of Eternal Life laid down by Christ. Let us place it alongside the definition of Science, and mark the points of contact. Uninterrupted correspondence with a perfect Environment is Eternal Life according to Science. "This is Life Eternal," said Christ, "that they may know Thee, the only true God, and Jesus Christ whom Thou has sent."[3] Life Eternal is to know God. To know God is to "correspond" with God. To correspond with God is to correspond with a Perfect Environment. And the organism which attains to this, in the nature of things must live for ever. Here is "eternal existence and eternal knowledge."

The main point of agreement between the scientific and the religious definition is that Life consists in a peculiar and personal relation defined as a "correspondence." This conception, that Life consists in correspondences, has been so abundantly

---

2 "Principles of Biology," p. 88.

3 John xvii.

illustrated already that it is now unnecessary to discuss it further. All Life indeed consists essentially in correspondences with various Environments. The artist's life is a correspondence with art; the musician's with music. To cut them off from these Environments is in that relation to cut off their Life. To be cut off from all Environment is death. To find a new Environment again and cultivate relation with it is to find a new Life. To live is to correspond, and to correspond is to live. So much is true in Science. But it is also true in Religion. And it is of great importance to observe that to Religion also the conception of Life is a correspondence. No truth of Christianity has been more ignorantly or wilfully travestied than the doctrine of Immortality. The popular idea, in spite of a hundred protests, is that Eternal Life is to live forever. A single glance at the *locus classicus*, might have made this error impossible. There we are told that Life Eternal is not to live. This is Life Eternal—*to know*. And yet—and it is a notorious instance of the fact that men who are opposed to Religion will take their conceptions of its profoundest truths from mere vuglar perversions—this view still represents to many cultivated men the Scriptural doctrine of Eternal Life. From time to time the taunt is thrown at Religion, not unseldom from lips which Science ought to have taught more caution, that the Future Life of Christianity is simply a prolonged existence, an eternal monotony, a blind and indefinite continuance of being. The Bible never could commit itself to any such empty platitude; nor could Christianity ever offer to the world a hope so colorless. Not that Eternal Life has nothing to do with everlastingness. That is part of the conception. And it is this aspect of the question that first arrests us in the field of Science. But even Science has more in its definition than longevity. It has a correspondence and an Environment; and although it cannot fill up these terms for Religion, it can indicate at least the nature of the relation, the kind of thing that is meant by Life. Science speaks to us indeed of much more than numbers of years. It defines degrees of Life. It explains a widening Environment. It unfolds the relation between a widening Environment and increasing complexity in organisms. And if it has no absolute contribution to the content of Religion, its analogies are not limited to a point. It yields to Immortality, and this is the most that Science can do in any case, the broad framework for a doctrine.

The further definition, moreover, of this correspondence as *knowing* is in the highest degree significant. Is not this the precise quality in an Eternal correspondence which the analogies of Science would prepare us to look for? Longevity is associated with complexity. And complexity in organisms is manifested by the successive addition of correspondences, each richer and larger than those which have gone before. The differentiation, therefore, of the spiritual organism ought to be signalized by the addition of the highest possible correspondence. It is not essential to the idea that the correspondence should be altogether novel; it is necessary rather that it should not. An altogether new correspondence appearing suddenly without shadow or prophecy would be a violation of continuity. What we should expect would be something new, and yet something that we were already prepared for. We should look for a further development in harmony with current developments; the extension of the last and highest correspondence in a new and higher direction. And this is exactly what we have. In the world with which biology deals, Evolution culminates in Knowledge.

At whatever point in the zoological scale this correspondence, or set of correspondences, begins, it is certain there is nothing higher. In its stunted infancy merely, when we meet with its rudest beginnings in animal intelligence, it is a thing so wonderful, as to strike every thoughtful and reverent observer with awe. Even among the invertebrates so marvellously are these or kindred powers displayed, that naturalists do not hesitate now, on the ground of intelligence at least, to classify some of the humblest creatures next to man himself.[4] Nothing

---

4 *Vide* Sir John Lubbock's "Ants, Bees, and Wasps," pp. 1, 181.

in nature, indeed, is so unlike the rest of nature, so prophetic of what is beyond it, so supernatural. And as manifested in Man who crowns creation with his all-embracing consciousness, there is but one word to describe his knowledge; it is Divine. If then from this point there is to be any further Evolution, this surely must be the correspondence in which it shall take place? This correspondence is great enough to demand development; and yet it is little enough to need it. The magnificence of what it has achieved relatively, is the pledge of the possibility of more; the insignificance of its conquest absolutely involves the probability of still richer triumphs. If anything, in short, in humanity is to go on it must be this. Other correspondences may continue likewise; others, again, we can well afford to leave behind. But this cannot cease. This correspondence—or this set of correspondences, for it is very complex—is it not that to which men with one consent would attach Eternal Life? Is there anything else to which they would attach it? Is anything better conceivable, anything worthier, fuller, nobler, anything which would represent a higher form of Evolution or offer a more perfect ideal for an Eternal Life?

But these are questions of quality; and the moment we pass from quantity to quality we leave Science behind. In the vocabulary of Science, Eternity is only the fraction of a word. It means mere everlastingness. To Religion, on the other hand, Eternity has little to do with time. To correspond with the God of Science, the Eternal Unknowable, would be everlasting existence; to correspond with "the true God and Jesus Christ," is Eternal Life. The quality of the Eternal Life alone makes the heaven; mere everlastingness might be no boon. Even the brief span of the temporal life is too long for those who spend its years in sorrow. Time itself, let alone Eternity, is all but excruciating to Doubt. And many besides Schopenhauer have secretly regarded consciousness as the hideous mistake and malady of Nature. Therefore we must not only have quantity of years, to speak in the language of the present, but quality of correspondence.

When we leave Science behind, this correspondence also receives a higher name. It becomes communion. Other names there are for it, religious and theological. It may be included in a general expression, Faith; or we may call it by a personal and specific term, Love. For the knowing of a Whole so great involves the co-operation of many parts.

Communion with God—can it be demonstrated in terms of Science that this is a correspondence which will never break? We do not appeal to Science for such a testimony. We have asked for its conception of an Eternal Life; and we have received for answer that Eternal Life would consist in a correspondence which should never cease, with an Environment which should never pass away. And yet what would Science demand of a perfect correspondence that is not met by this, *the knowing of God?* There is no other correspondence which could satisfy one at least of the conditions. Not one could be named which would not bear on the face of it the mark and pledge of its mortality. But this, to know God, stands alone. To know God, to be linked with God, to be linked with Eternity—if this is not the "eternal existence" of biology, what can more nearly approach it? And yet we are still a great way off—to establish a communication with the Eternal is not to secure Eternal Life. It must be assumed that the communication could be sustained. And to assume this would be to beg the question. So that we have still to prove Eternal Life. But let it be again repeated, we are not here seeking proofs. We are seeking light. We are merely reconnoitering from the furthest promontory of Science if so be that through the haze we may discern the outline of a distant coast and come to some conclusion as to the possibility of landing.

But, it may be replied, it is not open to any one handling the question of Immortality from the side of Science to remain neutral as to the question of fact. It is not enough to announce that he has no addition to make to the positive argument. This may be permitted with reference to other points of contact between Science and Religion, but not with this. We are told this question is settled—that there is no positive side. Science meets the entire conception of Immortality with a direct negative. In the face of a powerful consensus against even the possibility of a Future Life, to content oneself with saying that Science pretended to no argument in favor of it would be at once impertinent and dishonest. We must therefore devote ourselves for a moment to the question of possibility.

The problem is, with a material body and a mental organization inseparably connected with it, to bridge the grave. Emotion, volition, thought itself, are functions of the brain. When the brain is impaired, they are impaired. When the brain is not, they are not. Everything ceases with the dissolution of the material fabric; muscular activity and mental activity perish alike. With the pronounced positive statements on this point from many departments of modern Science we are all familiar. The fatal verdict is recorded by a hundred hands and with scarcely a shadow of qualification. "Unprejudiced philosophy is compelled to reject the idea of an individual immortality and of a personal continuance after death. With the decay and dissolution of its material substratum, through which alone it has acquired a conscious existence and become a person, and upon which it was dependent, the spirit must cease to exist."[5] To the same effect, Vogt: "Physiology decides definitely and categorically against individual immortality, as against any special existence of the soul. The soul does not enter the foetus like the evil spirit into persons possessed, but is a product of the development of the brain, just as muscular activity is a product of muscular development, and secretion a product of glandular development." After a careful review of the position of recent Science with regard to the whole doctrine, Mr. Graham sums up thus: "Such is the argument of Science, seemingly decisive against a future Life. As we listen to her array of syllogisms, our hearts die within us. The hopes of men, placed in one scale to be weighed, seem to fly up

---

5 Büchner: "Force and Matter," 3d ed., p. 232.

against the massive weight of her evidence, placed in the other. It seems as if all our arguments were vain and unsubstantial, as if our future expectations were the foolish dreams of children, as if there could not be any other possible verdict arrived at upon the evidence brought forward." [6]

Can we go on in the teeth of so real an obstruction? Has not our own weapon turned against us, Science abolishing with authoritative hand the very truth we are asking it to define?

What the philosopher has to throw into the other scale can be easily indicated. Generally speaking, he demurs to the dogmatism of the conclusion. That mind and brain react, that the mental and the physiological processes are related, and very intimately related, is beyond controversy. But how they are related, he submits, is still altogether unknown. The correlation of mind and brain do not involve their identity. And not a few authorities accordingly have consistently hesitated to draw any conclusion at all. Even Büchner's statement turns out, on close examination, to be tentative in the extreme. In prefacing his chapter on Personal Continuance, after a single sentence on the dependence of the soul and its manifestations upon a material substratum, he remarks, "Though we are unable to form a definite idea as to the *how* of this connection, we are still by these facts justified in asserting, that the mode of this connection renders it *apparently* impossible that they should continue to exist separately." [7] There is, therefore, a flaw at this point in the argument for materialism. It may not help the spiritualist in the least degree positively. He may be as far as ever from a theory of how consciousness could continue without the material tissue. But his contention secures for him the right of speculation. The path beyond may lie in hopeless gloom; but it is not barred. He may bring forward his theory if he will. And this is something. For a permission to go

---

6 "The Creed of Science," p. 169.

7 "Force and Matter," p. 231.

on is often the most that Science can grant to Religion.

Men have taken advantage of this loophole in various ways. And though it cannot be said that these speculations offer us more than a probability, this is still enough to combine with the deep-seated expectation in the bosom of mankind and give fresh lustre to the hope of a future life. Whether we find relief in the theory of a simple dualism; whether with Ulrici we further define the soul as an invisible enswathement of the body, material yet non-atomic; whether, with the "Unseen Universe," we are helped by the spectacle of known forms of matter shading off into an evergrowing subtilty, mobility, and immateriality; or whether, with Wundt, we regard the soul as "the ordered unity of many elements," it is certain that shapes can be given to the conception of a correspondence which shall bridge the grave such as to satisfy minds too much accustomed to weigh evidence to put themselves off with fancies.

But whether the possibilities of physiology or the theories of philosophy do or do not substantially assist us in realizing Immortality, is to Religion, to Religion at least regarded from the present point of view, of inferior moment. The fact of Immortality rests for us on a different basis. Probably, indeed, after all the Christian philosopher never engaged himself in a more superfluous task than in seeking along physiological lines to find room for a soul. The theory of Christianity has only to be fairly stated to make manifest its thorough independence of all the usual speculations on immortality. The theory is not that thought, volition, or emotion, as such are to survive the grave. The difficulty of holding a doctrine is this form, in spite of what has been advanced to the contrary, in spite of the hopes and wishes of mankind, in spite of all the scientific and philosophical attempts to make it tenable, is still profound. No secular theory of personal continuance, as even Butler acknowledged, does not equally demand the eternity of the brute. No secular theory defines the point in the chain of Evolution at which organisms become endowed with Immortality. No secular theory explains the condition of the endowment, nor indicates its goal. And if we have nothing more to fan hope than the unexplored mystery of the whole region, or the unknown remainders among the potencies of Life, then, as those who have "hope only in this world," we are "of all men the most miserable."

When we turn, on the other hand, to the doctrine as it came from the lips of Christ, we find ourselves in an entirely different region. He makes no attempt to project the material into the immaterial. The old elements, however refined and subtle as to their matter, are not in themselves to inherit the Kingdom of God. That which is flesh is flesh. Instead of attaching Immortality to the natural organism, He introduces a new and original factor which none of the secular, and few even of the theological theories, seem to take sufficiently into account. To Christanity, "he that hath the Son of God hath Life, and he that hath not the Son hath not Life." This, as we take it, defines the correspondence which is to bridge the grave. This is the clue to the nature of the Life that lies at the back of the spiritual organism. And this is the true solution of the mystery of Eternal Life.

There lies a something at the back of the correspondences of the spiritual organism—just as there lies a something at the back of the natural correspondence. To say that Life is a correspondence is only to express the partial truth. There is something behind. Life manifests itself in correspondences. But what determines them? The organism exhibits a variety of correspondences. What organizes them? As in the natural, so in the spiritual, there is a Principle of Life. We cannot get rid of that term. However clumsy, however provisional, however much a mere cloak for ignorance, Science as yet is unable to dispense with the idea of a Principle of Life. We must work with the word till we get a better. Now that which determines the correspondence of the spiritual organism is a Principle of Spiritual Life. It is a new and Divine Possession. He that hath the Son hath Life; conversely, he that hath Life hath the Son. And this indicates at once the quality and the quantity of the correspondence which is to bridge the grave. He that hath Life hath *the Son*. He possesses the Spirit of the Son. That Spirit is, so to speak, organized within him by the Son. It is the manifestation of the new nature—of which more anon. The fact to note at present is that this is not an organic correspondence, but a spiritual correspondence. It comes not from generation, but from regeneration. The relation between the spiritual man and his Environment is, in theological language, a filial relation. With the new Spirit, the filial correspondence, he knows the Father and this is Life Eternal. This is not only the real relation, but the only possible relation: "Neither knoweth any man the Father save the Son, and he to whomsoever the Son will reveal Him." And this on purely natural grounds. It takes the Divine to know the Divine—but in no more mysterious sense than it takes the human to understand the human. The analogy, indeed, for the whole field here has been finely expressed already by Paul: "What man," he asks, "knoweth the things of a man, save the spirit of man which is in him? even so the things of God knoweth no man, but the Spirit of God. Now we have received, not the spirit of the world, but the Spirit which is of God; that we might know the things that are freely given to us of God."[8]

It were idle, such being the quality of the new relation, to add that this also contains the guarantee of its eternity. Here at last is a correspondence which will never cease. Its powers in bridging the grave have been tried. The correspondence of the spiritual man possesses the supernatural virtues of the Resurrection and the Life. It is known by former experiment to have survived the "changes in the physical state of the environment," and those "mechanical actions" and "variations of available food," which Mr. Herbert Spencer tells us are "liable to stop the processes going on in the organism." In short, this is a correspondence which at once satisfies the demands of Science and Religion. In mere quantity it is different from every other correspondence known. Setting aside everything else in Religion, everything

---

8   1 Cor. ii. 11, 12.

adventitious, local, and provisional; dissecting into the bone and marrow we find this—a correspondence which can never break with an Environment which can never change. Here is a relation established with Eternity. The passing years lay no limiting hand on it. Corruption injures it not. It survives Death. It, and it only, will stretch beyond the grave and be found inviolate—

> "When the moon is old,
> And the stars are cold,
> And the books of the Judgment-day unfold."

The misgiving which will creep sometimes over the brightest faith has already received its expression and its rebuke: "Who shall separate us from the love of Christ? Shall tribulation, or distress, or persecution, or famine, or nakedness, or peril, or sword?" Shall these "changes in the physical state of the environment" which threaten death to the natural man destroy the spiritual? Shall death, or life, or angels, or principalities, or powers, arrest or tamper with his eternal correspondences? "Nay, in all these things we are more than conquerors through Him that loved us. For I am persuaded that neither death, nor life, nor angels, nor principalities, nor powers, nor things present, nor things to come, nor height, nor depth, nor any other creature, shall be able to separate us from the love of God, which is in Christ Jesus our Lord." [9]

It may seem an objection to some that the "perfect correspondence" should come to man in so extraordinary a way. The earlier stages in the doctrine are promising enough; they are entirely in line with Nature. And if Nature had also furnished the "perfect correspondence" demanded for an Eternal Life the position might be unassailable. But this sudden reference to a something outside the natural Environment destroys the continuity, and discovers a permanent weakness in the

---

9 Rom. viii. 35-39.

whole theory?

To which there is a twofold reply. In the first place, to go outside what we call Nature is not to go outside Environment. Nature, the natural Environment, is only a part of Environment. There is another large part which, though some profess to have no correspondence with it, is not on that account unreal, or even unnatural. The mental and moral world is unknown to the plant. But it is real. It cannot be affirmed either that it is unnatural to the plant; although it might be said that from the point of view of the Vegetable Kingdom it was *supernatural*. Things are natural or supernatural simply according to where one stands. Man is supernatural to the mineral; God is supernatural to the man. When a mineral is seized upon by the living plant and elevated to the organic kingdom, no tresspass against Nature is committed. It merely enters a larger Environment, which before was supernatural to it, but which now is entirely natural. When the heart of a man, again, is seized upon by the quickening Spirit of God, no further violence is done to natural law. It is another case of the inorganic, so to speak, passing into the organic.

But, in the second place, it is complained as if it were an enormity in itself that the spiritual correspondence should be furnished from the spiritual world. And to this the answer lies in the same direction. Correspondence in any case is the gift of Environment. The natural Environment gives men their natural faculties; the spiritual affords them their spiritual faculties. It is natural for the spiritual Environment to supply the spiritual faculties; it would be quite unnatural for the natural Environment to do it. The natural law of Biogenesis forbids it; the moral fact that the finite cannot comprehend the Infinite is against it; the spiritual principle that flesh and blood cannot inherit the kingdom of God renders it absurd. Not, however, that the spiritual faculties are, as it were, manufactured in the spiritual world and supplied ready-made to the spiritual organism—forced upon it as an external equipment. This certainly is not involved in saying that the spiritual faculties are furnished by the spiritual world. Organisms are not added to by accretion, as in the case of minerals, but by growth. And the spiritual faculties are organized in the spiritual protoplasm of the soul, just as other faculties are organized in the protoplasm of the body. The plant is made of materials which have once been inorganic. An organizing principle not belonging to their kingdom lays hold of them and elaborates them until they have correspondences with the kingdom to which the organizing principle belonged. Their original organizing principle, if it can be called by this name, was Crystallization; so that we have now a distinctly foreign power organizing in totally new and higher directions. In the spiritual world, similarly, we find an organizing principle at work among the materials of the organic kingdom, per forming a further miracle, but not a different kind of miracle, producing organizations of a novel kind, but not by a novel method. The second process, in fact, is simply what an enlightened evolutionist would have expected from the first. It marks the natural and legitimate progress of the development. And this in the line of the true Evolution—not the *linear* Evolution, which would look for the development of the natural man through powers already inherent, as if one were to look to Crystallization to accomplish the development of the mineral into the plant,—but that larger form of Evolution which includes among its factors the double Law of Biogenesis and the immense further truth that this involves.

What is further included in this complex correspondence we shall have opportunity to illustrate afterwards.[10] Meantime let it be noted on what the Christian argument for Immortality really rests. It stands upon the pedestal on which the theologian rests the whole of historical Christianity—the Resurrection of Jesus Christ.

It ought to be placed in the forefront of all Christian teaching that Christ's mission on earth was to give men Life. "I am come," He said, "that ye might have Life, and that ye might

---

10 *Vide* "Conformity to Type," page 287.

have it more abundantly." And that He meant literal Life, literal spiritual and Eternal Life, is clear from the whole course of His teaching and acting. To impose a metaphorical meaning on the commonest word of the New Testament is to violate every canon of interpretation, and at the same time to charge the greatest of teachers with persistently mystifying His hearers by an unusual use of so exact a vehicle for expressing definite thought as the Greek language, and that on the most momentous subject of which He ever spoke to men. It is a canon of interpretation, according to Alford, that "a figurative sense of words is never admissible except when required by the context." The context, in most cases, is not only directly unfavorable to a figurative meaning, but in innumerable instances in Christ's teaching Life is broadly contrasted with Death. In the teaching of the apostles, again, we find that, without exception, they accepted the term in its simple literal sense. Reuss defines the apostolic belief with his usual impartiality when—and the quotation is doubly pertinent here—he discovers in the apostle's conception of Life, first, "the idea of a real existence, an existence such as is proper to God and to the Word; an imperishable existence—that is to say, not subject to the vicissitudes and imperfections of the finite world. This primary idea is repeatedly expressed, at least in a negative form; it leads to a doctrine of immortality, or, to speak more correctly, of life, far surpassing any that had been expressed in the formulas of the current philosophy or theology, and resting upon premises and conceptions altogether different. In fact, it can dispense both with the philosophical thesis of the immateriality or indestructibility of the human soul, and with the theologicial thesis of a miraculous corporeal reconstruction of our person; theses, the first of which is altogether foreign to the religion of the Bible, and the second absolutely opposed to reason." Second, "the idea of life, as it is conceived in this system, implies the idea of a power, an operation, a communication, since this life no longer remains, so to speak, latent or passive in God and in the Word, but through them reaches the believer. It is not a mental somnolent thing; it is not a plant without fruit; it is a germ which is to find fullest development."[11]

If we are asked to define more clearly what is meant by this mysterious endowment of Life, we again hand over the difficulty to Science. When Science can define the Natural Life and the Physical Force we may hope for further clearness on the nature and action of the Spiritual Powers. The effort to detect the living Spirit must be at least as idle as the attempt to subject protoplasm to microscopic examination in the hope of discovering Life. We are warned, also, not to expect too much. "Thou canst not tell whence it cometh or whither it goeth." This being its quality, when the Spiritual Life is discovered in the laboratory it will possibly be time to give it up altogether. It may say, as Socrates of his soul, "You may bury me—if you can catch me."

Science never corroborates a spiritual truth without illuminating it. The threshold of Eternity is a place where many shadows meet. And the light of Science here, where everything is so dark, is welcome a thousand times. Many men would be religious if they knew where to begin; many would be more religious if they were sure where it would end. It is not indifference that keeps some men from God, but ignorance. "Good Master, what must I do to inherit Eternal Life?" is still the deepest question of the age. What is Religion? What am I to believe? What seek with all my heart and soul and mind?—this is the imperious question sent up to consciousness from the depths of being in all earnest hours; sent down again, alas, with many of us, time after time, unanswered. Into all our thought and work and reading this question pursues us. But the theories are rejected one by one; the great books are returned sadly to their shelves, the years pass, and the problem remains unsolved. The confusion of tongues here is terrible. Every day a new authority announces himself. Poets, philosophers, preachers, try their

---

11 "History of Christian Theology in the Apostolic Age,"
  vol. ii. p. 496.

hand on us in turn. New prophets arise, and beseech us for our soul's sake to give ear to them—at last in an hour of inspiration they have discovered the final truth. Yet the doctrine of yesterday is challenged by a fresh philosophy to-day; and the creed of to-day will fall in turn before the criticism of to-morrow. Increase of knowledge increaseth sorrow. And at length the conflicting truths, like the beams of light in the laboratory experiment, combine in the mind to make total darkness.

But here are two outstanding authorities agreed—not men, not philosophers, not creeds. Here is the voice of God and the voice of Nature. I cannot be wrong if I listen to them. Sometimes when uncertain of a voice from its very loudness, we catch the missing syllable in the echo. In God and Nature we have Voice and Echo. When I hear both, I am assured. My sense of hearing does not betray me twice. I recognize the Voice in the Echo, the Echo makes me certain of the Voice; I listen and I know. The question of a Future Life is a biological question. Nature may be silent on other problems of Religion; but here she has a right to speak. The whole confusion around the doctrine of Eternal Life has arisen from making it a question of Philosophy. We shall do ill to refuse a hearing to any speculation of Philosophy; the ethical relations here especially are intimate and real. But in the first instance Eternal Life, as a question of *Life*, is a problem for Biology. The soul is a living organism. And for any question as to the soul's Life we must appeal to Life-science. And what does the Life-science teach? That if I am to inherit Eternal Life, I must cultivate a correspondence with the Eternal. This is a simple proposition, for Nature is always simple. I take this proposition, and, leaving Nature, proceed to fill it in. I search everywhere for a clue to the Eternal. I ransack literature for a definition of a correspondence between man and God. Obviously that can only come from one source. And the analogies of Science permit us to apply to it. All knowledge lies in Environment. When I want to know about minerals I go to minerals. When I want to know about flowers I go to flowers. And they tell me. In their own way they speak to me, each in its own way, and each for itself—not the mineral for the flower, which is impossible, nor the flower for the mineral, which is also impossible. So if I want to know about Man, I go to his part of the Environment. And he tells me about himself, not as the plant or the mineral, for he is neither, but in his own way. And if I want to know about God, I go to His part of the Environment. And he tells me about Himself, not as a Man, for He is not Man, but in His own way. And just as naturally as the flower and the mineral and the Man, each in their own way, tell me about themselves, He tells me about Himself. He very strangely condescends indeed in making things plain to me, actually assuming for a time the Form of a Man that I at my poor level may better see Him. This is my opportunity to know Him. This incarnation is God making Himself accessible to human thought—God opening to man the possibility of correspondence through Jesus Christ. And this correspondence and this Environment are those I seek. He Himself assures me, "This is Life Eternal, that they might know Thee, the only true God, and Jesus Christ whom Thou has sent." Do I not now discern the deeper meaning in *"Jesus Christ whom Thou has sent?"* Do I not better understand with what vision and rapture the profoundest of the disciples exclaims, "The Son of God is come, and hath given us an understanding that we might know Him that is True?" [12]

Having opened correspondence with the Eternal Environment, the subsequent stages are in the line of all other normal development. We have but to continue, to deepen, to extend, and to enrich the correspondence that has been begun. And we shall soon find to our surprise that this is accompanied by another and parallel process. The action is not all upon our side. The Environment also will be found to correspond. The influence of Environment is one of the greatest and most substantial of modern biological doctrines. Of the power of Environment to

---

12 1 John v. 20.

form or transform organisms, of its ability to develop or suppress function, of its potency in determining growth, and generally of its immense influence in Evolution, there is no need now to speak. But Environment is now acknowledged to be one of the most potent factors in the Evolution of Life. The influence of Environment, too, seems to increase rather than diminish as we approach the higher forms of being. The highest forms are the most mobile; their capacity of change is the greatest; they are, in short, most easily acted on by Environment. And not only are the highest organisms the most mobile, but the highest parts of the highest organisms are more mobile than the lower. Environment can do little, comparatively, in the direction of inducing variation in the body of a child; but how plastic is its mind! How infinitely sensitive is its soul! How infallibly can it be tuned to music or to dissonance by the moral harmony or discord of its outward lot! How decisively indeed are we not all formed and moulded, made or unmade, by external circumstance! Might we not all confess with Ulysses,—

"I am a part of all that I have met?"

Much more, then, shall we look for the influence of Environment on the spiritual nature of him who has opened correspondence with God. Reaching out his eager and quickened faculties to the spiritual world around him, shall he not become spiritual? In vital contact with Holiness, shall he not become holy? Breathing now an atmosphere of ineffable Purity, shall he miss becoming pure? Walking with God from day to day, shall he fail to be taught of God?

Growth in grace is sometimes described as a strange, mystical, and unintelligible process. It is mystical, but neither strange nor unintelligible. It proceeds according to Natural Law, and the leading factor in sanctification is Influence of Environment. The possibility of it depends upon the mobility of the organism; the result, on the extent and frequency of certain correspondences.

These facts insensibly lead on to further suggestion. Is it not possible that these biological truths may carry with them the clue to a still profounder philosophy—even that of Regeneration?

Evolutionists tell us that by the influence of environment certain aquatic animals have become adapted to a terrestrial mode of life. Breathing normally by gills, as the result and reward of a continued effort carried on from generation to generation to inspire the air of heaven direct, they have slowly acquired the lung-function. In the young organism, true to the ancestral type, the gill still persists—as in the tadpole of the common frog. But as maturity approaches, the true lung appears; the gill gradually transfers its task to the higher organ. It then becomes atrophied and disappears, and finally respiration in the adult is conducted by lungs alone.[13] We may be far, in the meantime, from saying that this is proved. It is for those who accept it to deny the justice of the spiritual analogy. Is religion to them unscientific in its doctrine of Regeneration? Will the evolutionist who admits the regeneration of the frog under the modifying influence of a continued correspondence with a new environment, care to question the possibility of the soul acquiring such a faculty as that of Prayer, the marvellous breathing-function of the new creature, when in contact with the atmosphere of a besetting God? Is the change from the earthly to the heavenly more mysterious than the change from the aquatic to the terrestrial mode of life? Is Evolution to stop with the organic? If it be objected that it has taken ages to perfect the function in the batrachian, the reply is, that it will take ages to perfect the function in the Christian. For every thousand years the natural evolution will allow for the development of its organism, the Higher Biology will grant its product millions. We have indeed spoken of the spiritual correspondence as already perfect—but it is perfect only as

---

13 *Vide* also the remarkable experiments of Fräulein v. Chauvin on the Transformation of the Mexican Axoloti into Amblystoma.—Weismann's "Studies in the Theory of Descent," vol. ii. pt. iii.

the bud is perfect. "It doth not yet appear what it shall be," any more than it appeared a million years ago what the evolving batrachian would be.

But to return. We have been dealing with the scientific aspects of communion with God. Insensibly, from quantity we have been led to speak of quality. And enough has now been advanced to indicate generally the nature of that correspondence with which is necessarily associated Eternal Life. There remain but one or two details to which we must lastly, and very briefly, address ourselves.

The quality of everlastingness belongs, as we have seen, to a single correspondence, or rather to a single set of correspondences. But it is apparent that before this correspondence can take full and final effect a further process is necessary. By some means it must be separated from all the other correspondences of the organism which do not share its peculiar quality. In this life it is restrained by these other correspondences. They may contribute to it, or hinder it; but they are essentially of a different order. They belong not to Eternity but to Time, and to this present world; and, unless some provision is made for dealing with them, they will detain the aspiring organism in this present world till Time is ended. Of course, in a sense, all that belongs to Time belongs also to Eternity; but these lower correspondences are in their nature unfitted for an Eternal Life. Even if they were perfect in their relation to their Environment, they would still not be Eternal. However opposed, apparently, to the scientific definition of Eternal Life, it is yet true that perfect correspondence with Environment is not Eternal Life. A very important word in the complete definition is, in this sentence, omitted. On that word it has not been necessary hitherto, and for obvious reasons, to place any emphasis, but when we come to deal with false pretenders to Immortality we must return to it. Were the definition complete as it stands, it might, with the permission of the psycho-physiologist, guarantee the Immortality of every living thing. In the dog, for instance, the material framework giving way at death might leave the released canine spirit still free to inhabit the old Environment. And so with every creature which had ever established a conscious relation with surrounding things. Now the difficulty in framing a theory of Eternal Life has been to construct one which will exclude the brute creation, drawing the line rigidly at man, or at least somewhere within the human race. Not that we need object to the Immortality of the dog, or of the whole inferior creation. Nor that we need refuse a place to any intelligible speculation which would people the earth to-day with the invisible forms of all things that have ever lived. Only we still insist that this is not Eternal Life. And why? Because their Environment is not Eternal. Their correspondence, however firmly established, is established with that which shall pass away. An Eternal Life demands an Eternal Environment.

The demand for a perfect Environment as well as for a perfect correspondence is less clear in Mr. Herbert Spencer's definition than it might be. But it is an essential factor. An organism might remain true to its Environment, but what if the Environment played it false? If the organism possessed the power to change, it could adapt itself to successive changes in the Environment. And if this were guaranteed we should also have the conditions for Eternal Life fulfilled. But what if the Environment passed away altogether? What if the earth swept suddenly into the sun? This is a change of Environment against which there could be no precaution and for which there could be as little provision. With a changing Environment even, there must always remain the dread and possibility of a falling out of correspondence. At the best, Life would be uncertain. But with a changeless Environment—such as that possessed by the spiritual organism—the perpetuity of the correspondence, so far as the external relation is concerned, is guaranteed. This quality of permanence in the Environment distinguishes the religious relation from every other. Why should not the musician's life be an Eternal Life? Because, for one thing, the musical world, the Environment with which he corresponds, is not eternal. Even if his correspondence in itself could last eternally, the environing material things with which he corresponds must pass away. His soul might last forever—but not his violin. So the man of the world might last forever—but not the world. His Environment is not eternal; nor are even his correspondences—the world passeth away *and the lust thereof.*

We find, then, that man, or the spiritual man, is equipped with two sets of correspondences. One set possesses the quality of everlastingness, the other is temporal. But unless these are separated by some means the temporal will continue to impair and hinder the eternal. The final preparation, therefore, for the inheriting of Eternal Life must consist in the abandonment of the non-eternal elements. These must be unloosed and dissociated from the higher elements. And this is effected by a closing catastrophe—Death.

Death ensues because certain relations in the organism are not adjusted to certain relations in the Environment. There will come a time in each history when the imperfect correspondences of the organism will betray themselves by a failure to compass some necessary adjustment. This is why Death is associated with Imperfection. Death is the necessary result of Imperfection, and the necessary end of it. Imperfect correspondence gives imperfect and uncertain Life. "Perfect correspondence," on the other hand, according to Mr. Herbert Spencer, would be "perfect Life." To abolish Death, therefore, all that would be necessary would be to abolish Imperfection. But it is the claim of Christianity that it can abolish Death. And it is significant to notice that it does so by meeting this very demand of Science—it abolishes Imperfection.

The part of the organism which begins to get out of correspondence with the Organic Environment is the only part which is in vital correspondence with it. Though a fatal disadvantage to the natural man to be thrown out of correspondence with this Environment, it is of inestimable importance to the spiritual man. For so long as it is maintained the way is barred for a further Evolution. And hence the condition necessary for the further Evolution is that the spiritual be released from the natural. That is to say, the condition of the further Evolution is Death. *Mora janua Vitæ*, therefore, becomes a scientific formula. Death, being the final sifting of all the correspondences, is the indispensable factor of the higher Life. In the language of Science, not less than of Scripture, "To die is gain."

The sifting of the correspondences is done by Nature. This is its last and greatest contribution to mankind. Over the mouth of the grave the perfect and the imperfect submit to their final separation. Each goes to its own—earth to earth, ashes to ashes, dust to dust, Spirit to Spirit. The dust shall return to the earth as it was; and the Spirit shall return unto God who gave it"

www.ingramcontent.com/pod-product-compliance
Lightning Source LLC
Chambersburg PA
CBHW022122090426
42743CB00008B/960